The Living Earth Part 4

Our planet

Christine Back

A & C Black · London

A & C Black (Publishers) Limited
35 Bedford Row, London WC1R 4JH

Filmset by August Filmsetting, Warrington, Cheshire
Printed in Hong Kong by Dai Nippon Printing Co. Ltd

Back, Christine
    The Living Earth.
    Part 4: Our planet
    1. Ecology—Juvenile literature
    I. Title
    508   QH541 4

    ISBN 0-7136-2269-5
    ISBN 0-7136-2270-9 Pbk

Acknowledgments

Artwork by B. L. Kearley Ltd.

Photographs
Pat and Helen Clay, pages 16, 17, 42, 57, 59, 63;
B. W. Hadley A.I.I.P, Royal Observatory
Edinburgh, Copyright © 1978, page 4; NASA,
page 5; Copyright Solarfilma Iceland, pages 8, 57;
The Slide Centre, page 7; Barnaby's Picture
Library, pages 8, 21, 43; John and Penny Hubley,
page 11; Brian and Cherry Alexander, page 11;
British Tourist Authority, page 15; Chris Gough,
page 44; J. A. Friend, page 19; Aerofilms Ltd,
pages 19, 27; Crown, page 25; Ken Pilsbury
F.R.P.S. F.R.Met.S. page 20; Andrew Boon,
page 32; Royal National Lifeboat Institute, page 27;
Reproduced by permission of the Director
Institute of Geological Sciences (NERC), NERC
Copyright reserved/Crown Copyright reserved,
pages 33, 35, 45, 49, 51, 52, 53, 54; India Tourist
Office, page 36; G. A. MacDonald United States
Geological Survey, page 37; Geoscience Features,
page 38; P. W. Gardiner, Traveller's World,
page 39; Oxfam, page 40; Chris Fairclough, pages
52, 57; Farmer's Weekly, pages 55, 59; Liba
Taylor, pages 57, 59; John Powys, page 60;
M. Nimmo, page 19; Robert Madden, page 22;
Photograph by BP Oil Ltd, page 62; Barrie Watts,
cover, page 16 (top).

Cover: A rocky coast
Title page: Deciduous woodland

Contents

Our planet

Our planet earth belongs to a *solar system*. In a solar system, there are planets moving around a sun. Each planet may have one or more moons which move around it.

In our solar system, there are nine planets. The earth is one of them. The planets *orbit* the sun. This means that they travel in a circle around the sun. Planets have no light of their own. They receive light from their sun.

Astronomers study the stars using telescopes. They believe that there are many solar systems in space.

Astronomers believe that many of the stars are suns with solar systems of their own, but the planets are too small and far away to be seen by telescope.

Our planet earth moves around its sun. But there is also movement inside the earth and on its surface. All the time, new rocks are being made and old ones are worn away.

This book will help you to understand more about the planet on which we live and the solar system to which it belongs.

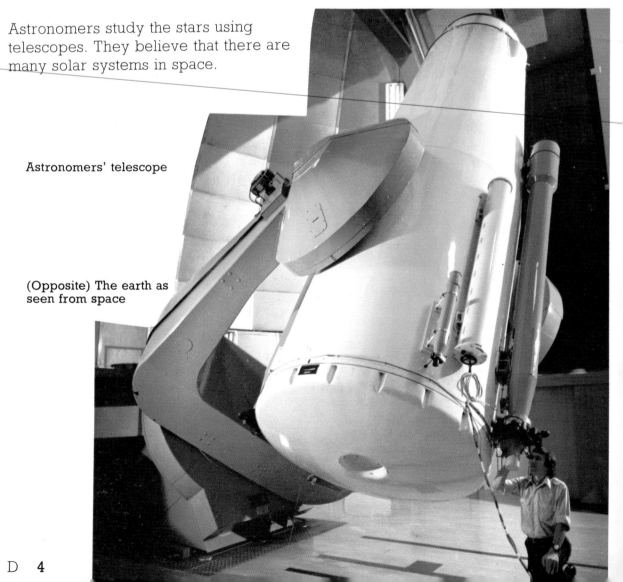

Astronomers' telescope

(Opposite) The earth as seen from space

Where is our planet?

Look at this diagram.

What are the names of the other planets in our solar system?

Which two planets orbit closer to the sun than the earth?

Which planet is furthest away from the sun?

Each planet in our solar system takes a different length of time to orbit the sun. A year is the time it takes for the earth to do this. One year is 365¼ days. But to make life easier, we say that a year is 365 days exactly. Once every four years we have a leap year, with 366 days, to make up for the extra quarter of a day.

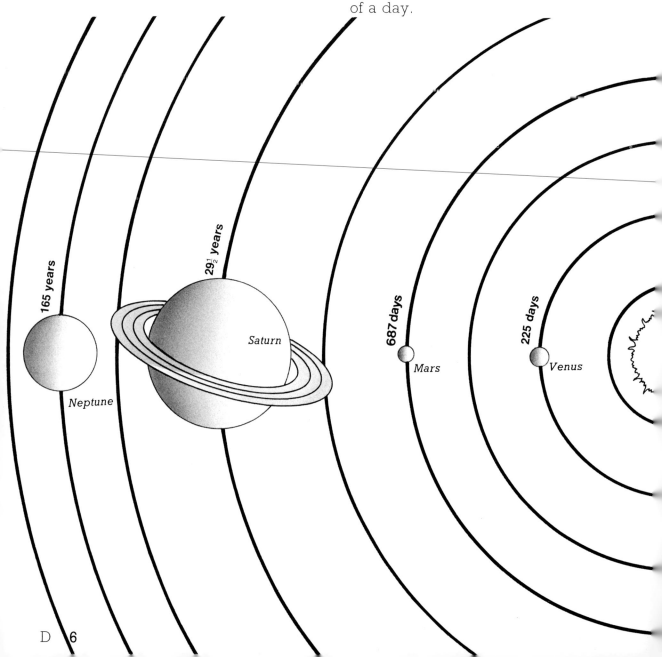

165 years

29½ years

Saturn

687 days

225 days

Neptune

Mars

Venus

Can you see the moon going around the earth? While the earth orbits the sun, the moon goes round the earth about once a month.

This diagram has been drawn very simply. It does not show how far apart the planets are. The earth is 150 million kilometres from the sun! Jupiter is the biggest planet and Mercury is the smallest. The sun is bigger than all the planets put together! The diagram shows our moon but we have left out all the other planets' moons. Jupiter has twelve moons.

What is the Sun?

The sun is a *star*. A star is a mass of hot gases. Have you ever stood close to a fire and felt its warmth? The sun is millions of miles away from us and yet we can still feel its heat. Imagine how big the sun must be for us to feel its heat from so far away. What do you think would happen to us if the sun stopped burning?

There would be no plants or animals on the earth without the sun. Living things need warmth, light and water to survive.

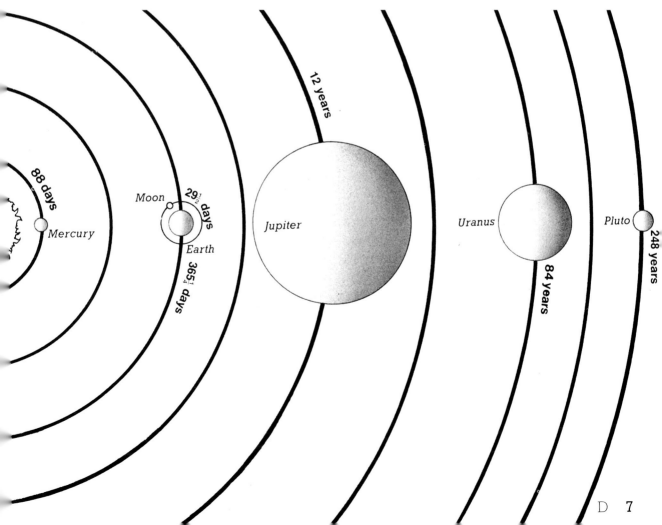

Night and day

The sun gives light as well as heat. Do we get light all the time? Has it been light, without a break, since this time yesterday? There are twenty-four hours in a day. Can you work out how many hours were light in the last twenty-four hours? Can you guess why you didn't see the sun all the time?

This diagram shows how the earth is spinning. Only the side facing the sun receives light. The other side is in darkness

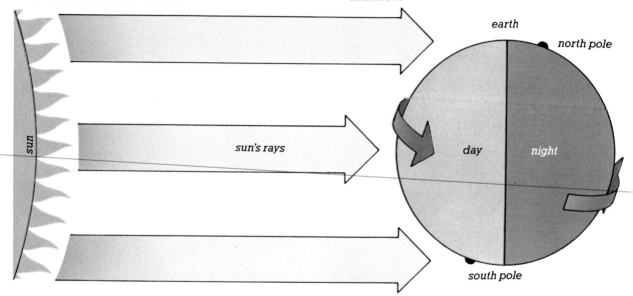

sun

sun's rays

earth

north pole

day   night

south pole

As the earth moves round the sun, it also spins like a top. The earth spins round once every twenty-four hours. During this time different parts of the earth face the sun and receive its light.

When one side of the earth is facing the sun, the other side is in darkness and gets cold. We say it is day when it is light and night when it is dark.

There are some parts of the world which face the sun both day and night. This happens near the North and South Poles when each is having summer. You can see the North and South Poles in the diagram above.

Midnight in Iceland, during summer

The moon shines at night – on the dark side of the earth. The light is not really from the moon. It is sunlight reflected from the moon. When the moon is shaded it does not give any reflected light.

Sometimes the earth shades the moon from the sun. Sometimes there are clouds between the earth and moon which stop us seeing its reflected light.

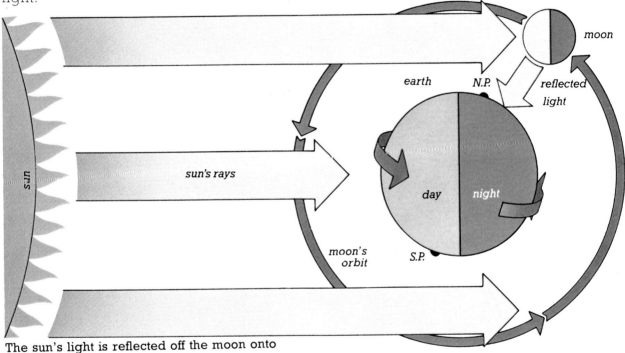

The sun's light is reflected off the moon onto the dark side of the earth

Eclipse of the sun

Sometimes the moon passes between the earth and the sun. This does not happen very often but when it does, there is an *eclipse* of the sun. The sun is hidden by the moon.

Try this

Look for the moon tonight. See if the sun is shining on it to light it up. See if there are clouds passing between you and the moon. If it is a clear night without clouds, you may see stars too. These stars are masses of hot gases like the sun. They look smaller because they are further away.

Try this

Keep a record of the night sky.
Draw the shape of the moon each night for thirty nights. Sometimes you may not be able to see it because of heavy cloud.

The shape of the moon will gradually change as the earth shades it from the sun. This chart shows you how to make the record, but you will need spaces for thirty nights and not just three.

date	Tues 3rd May	Wed 4th May	Thur 5th May
moon shape	○	—	◗
cloud cover	none	all over sky	patchy

The moon orbits the earth once every $29\frac{1}{2}$ days. This is called a *lunar month*. Lunar means 'to do with the moon'. Watch to see how far the moon travels every twenty-four hours. Look carefully at the stars. Are they all moving with the moon?

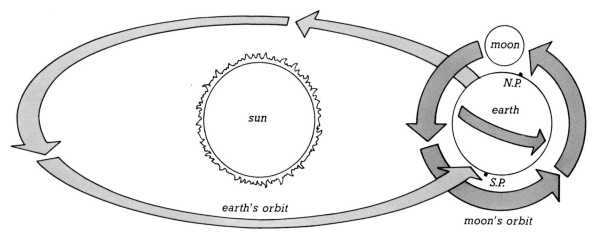

This diagram shows how the earth revolves and orbits the sun. It also shows how the moon orbits the earth

Climate

The earth is heated by the sun. Do you think all parts of the world have the same amount of heat from the sun all year round? Think about people going on holiday. They may need to travel abroad for a hot, sunny holiday. Or they may want a colder place with snow for ski-ing.

In this diagram, you can see that the sun's rays are more concentrated on the middle part of the earth's surface and more spread out over the top and bottom parts of the earth. This means that the middle part of the earth is the hottest and the top and bottom parts of the earth are the coldest. The other parts of the earth have temperatures between the two extremes.

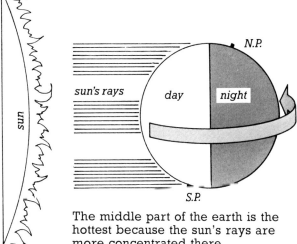

The middle part of the earth is the hottest because the sun's rays are more concentrated there.

Look at the clothes these people are wearing. Are they the same? Think what it would feel like to arrive in Jamaica wearing clothes from Greenland! People wear clothes to suit the climate they live in. Animals which live in cold countries have coats of thick hair, fur or wool to keep them warm in the same way.

Clothes in Greenland

Clothes in Jamaica

We can draw imaginary lines around the world to help us see where the hot and cold parts are. These lines have names. The earth above the *equator* (the imaginary line around the centre of the earth) is called the *Northern Hemisphere*. The earth below the equator is called the *Southern Hemisphere*.

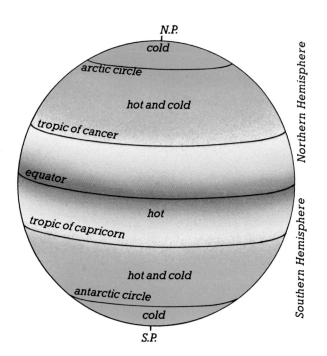

A globe is a model of the earth which shows us where each country is. When the imaginary lines are drawn on a globe, you can work out which are hot and which are cold countries.

Can you find the country you live in on a globe? Is your country in a part which is always hot, always cold, or hot and cold?

Look carefully at the globe pictures. You will see land and sea marked. The sea can be hot, cold, or sometimes hot and sometimes cold – just like the land.

Globe

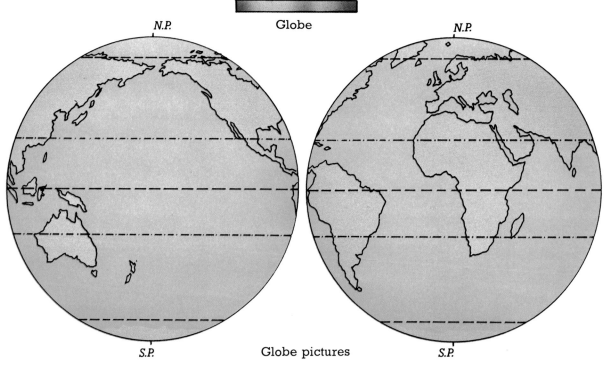

Globe pictures

The seasons

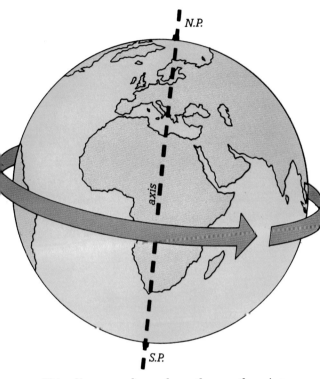

You know that some parts of the world are hotter than others. You also know that the sun can give direct heat and light only to the places which face it. You found your country on the globe. You worked out whether it was in a hot or cold part of the world, or in a place which is sometimes hot and sometimes cold. Think very carefully. Has there been the same amount of heat and light every day since this time last year?

The earth spins round an imaginary pole which goes through the middle of it. This is called the *axis*. The earth's axis is not upright, so the earth leans to one side as it spins. One hemisphere is tilted towards the sun and the other hemisphere is tilted away from the sun. The Northern Hemisphere always does the opposite from the Southern Hemisphere.

In the diagram below, the Southern Hemisphere is tilted towards the sun, so it receives more light and heat. The Northern Hemisphere is tilted away from the sun, so it receives less light and heat.

▲ This diagram shows how the earth spins round its axis. The pink arrow shows the direction in which the earth spins

▼ Because of the tilt of the earth's axis, one hemisphere receives more light and heat than the other.

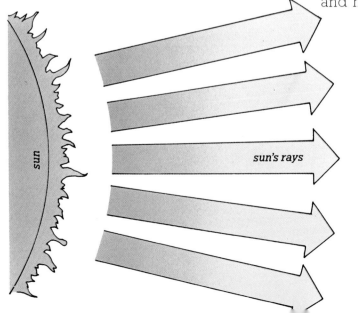

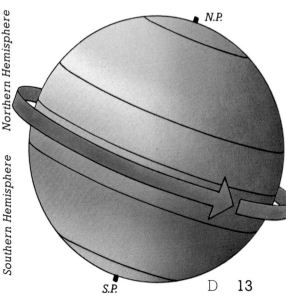

The earth's axis is always tilted the same way. But because the earth moves around the sun, different parts of the earth are tilted towards the sun at different times. This gives us the seasons – summer, autumn, winter and spring.

For some months of the year, the Northern Hemisphere is tilted towards the sun and the Southern Hemisphere is tilted away from the sun. During this time, the Northern Hemisphere gets more light and heat, so it is summer there. The Southern Hemisphere gets less light and heat, so it is winter there.

During other months, the Northern Hemisphere is tilted away from the sun Then it is winter in the Northern Hemisphere and summer in the Southern Hemisphere.

Near the North and South Poles, summer is warmer than winter, but it isn't hot. The sun is not strong enough to melt all the ice. The North and South Poles are the coldest parts of the earth.

In Trinidad, winter is nearly as hot as summer. Trinidad is near the equator. This is the hottest part of the earth.

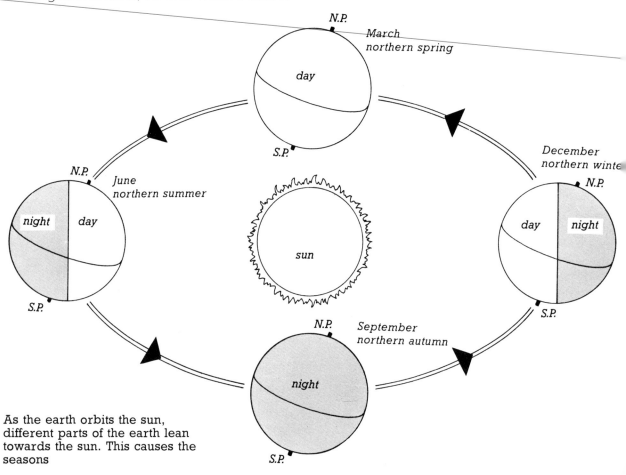

As the earth orbits the sun, different parts of the earth lean towards the sun. This causes the seasons

Between the very hot and very cold places are the places which are sometimes hot and sometimes cold, like the countries in Europe. When they are cold it is winter. When they are hot it is summer. People need to wear different types of clothes for the different seasons.

In these places, it gradually changes from winter to summer and from summer to winter. After winter, it begins to get warmer and there are more daylight hours. This is *spring*. At the end of summer, it gradually becomes colder and there are less daylight hours. This is *autumn*.

Different plants and other living creatures live in different parts of the world. Some are able to live in very hot conditions and others in very cold ones. But what about the places which are sometimes hot and sometimes cold? You know that people in these countries wear different clothes for different seasons. What do you think the plants and animals do? Many can live through all four seasons. They often grow and behave in different ways as the seasons change.

Summer in London

Winter in London

Spring is the beginning of the growing year. The weather begins to get warmer. New plants grow from seeds. Buds grow on existing plants. Inside the buds, there are new leaves, stems and flowers. Growing plants give extra food and shelter to animals. In spring, young creatures are born or hatch from eggs. Look at the bright colours in this picture.

Summer is the time when everything keeps growing and develops. There are flowers and fruits on the plants. The young creatures grow up. Compare this picture with the one for spring. Notice the colour changes and how everything has grown.

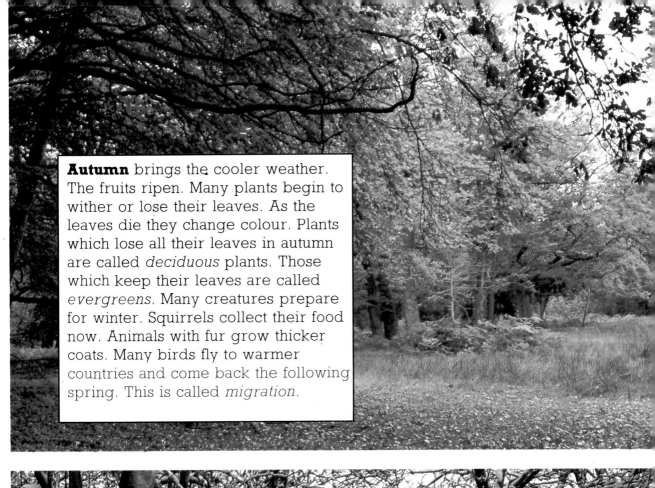

Autumn brings the cooler weather. The fruits ripen. Many plants begin to wither or lose their leaves. As the leaves die they change colour. Plants which lose all their leaves in autumn are called *deciduous* plants. Those which keep their leaves are called *evergreens*. Many creatures prepare for winter. Squirrels collect their food now. Animals with fur grow thicker coats. Many birds fly to warmer countries and come back the following spring. This is called *migration*.

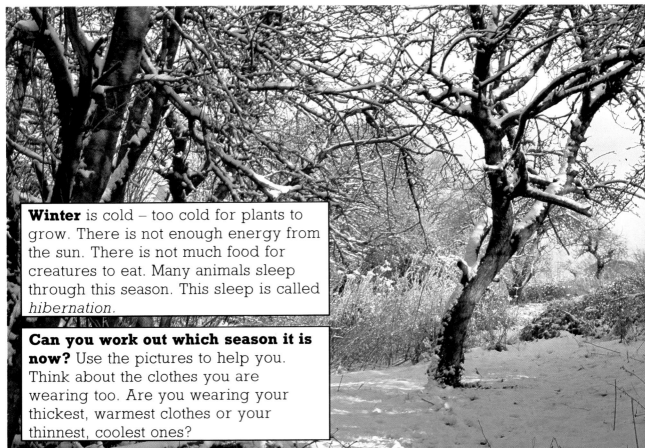

Winter is cold – too cold for plants to grow. There is not enough energy from the sun. There is not much food for creatures to eat. Many animals sleep through this season. This sleep is called *hibernation*.

Can you work out which season it is now? Use the pictures to help you. Think about the clothes you are wearing too. Are you wearing your thickest, warmest clothes or your thinnest, coolest ones?

Weather

If you were asked what the weather was like today, what would you say? You would probably say whether the sun was shining, whether or not it was raining – or perhaps snowing. You may say whether the wind was blowing and whether it was hot or cold. We know what weather is **like,** but have you ever thought about how it is caused?

Around the outside of the earth is a blanket of air which we call the *atmosphere*. The air is made of gases, like oxygen and carbon dioxide. (See *The Living Earth* – Part 1.) The atmosphere *insulates* the surface of the earth. This means that when the sun is not shining, the atmosphere reduces the amount of heat which is lost by the earth. The atmosphere also stops some of the sun's heat from reaching the earth.

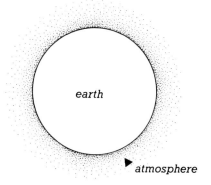

earth

▶ atmosphere

When water in rivers, lakes and the sea is warmed by the sun, a little of the water becomes *water vapour* and rises up into the atmosphere. This is called *evaporation*. Water vapour is invisible. When it cools, it becomes liquid water again. This is called *condensation*. (You can see water vapour condensing when you boil a kettle. The water vapour is cooled down by the air and it forms tiny drops of liquid water which we call steam.) *Humidity* is the word we use when we are measuring the amount of water vapour in the air.

Water vapour in the atmosphere can become dew, frost, mist or clouds.

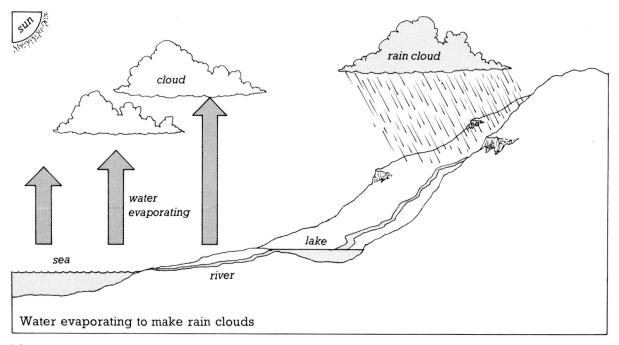

sun

cloud

rain cloud

water evaporating

lake

sea

river

Water evaporating to make rain clouds

Dew

Early in the mornings the ground is sometimes wet even though it hasn't rained. This water on the ground is called *dew*.

During the night, the earth cools. Because of this, the water vapour which is just above the ground condenses. The condensation forms dew.

Frost

If the night is very cold then *frost* forms on the ground. This is water vapour which froze as soon as it condensed. Tomorrow morning look outside as soon as you wake up. See if there is any dew or frost.

Mist

Mist is similar to steam and is caused by condensation. There is often a mist when the days are warm and the nights are cold. The air near the ground is colder than the air higher up. Water vapour near the ground condenses to form mist, but higher up the air is clear – as you can see in this photograph.

Clouds

When vapour rises in the atmosphere, it cools and collects together. Gradually the patches of vapour condense and become large enough to be seen. They become *clouds*. Clouds may be different shapes and different heights in the sky.

If the whole sky is covered with cloud we say it is *overcast*. When it is very cloudy less heat from the sun reaches us and the weather becomes colder. Eventually clouds release their water as rain, hail or snow. It is usually only in winter that snow reaches the ground before melting.

Cirrus clouds

Cumulus clouds

Stratus clouds

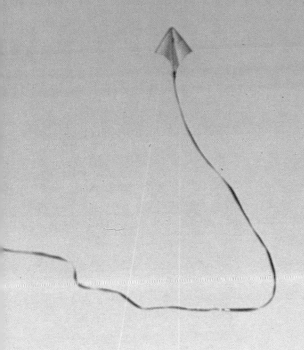

Wind

Wind is moving air. The reasons why air moves from one place to another are very complicated. The heating up and cooling down of air is part of what happens. The rotation of the earth is also partly responsible for the movement of the air.

We cannot see wind, but we can feel it blowing against us. We can also see the wind blowing things around us – plants sway in the wind, waves ripple on water and smoke from fires is blown across the sky. Some winds blow near the earth's surface. They carry most of the clouds. Other winds blow higher in the atmosphere. Some of these are called *jet streams*. These are the winds flown through by aeroplanes which fly above the clouds.

Winds blow at different strengths as well as at different heights. The faster the wind is moving, the stronger it is. A slow wind is a *breeze* and a fast one is a *gale.* Strong winds can cause a great deal of damage. The most dangerous winds blow in the tropical areas of the world between the Tropic of Cancer and the Tropic of Capricorn. These winds are called *hurricanes* and are strong enough to blow down houses and uproot trees.

Tornadoes are also extremely strong winds. They blow in certain parts of the world, especially in the United States of America. Tornadoes blow in a circle in a small area. Everything nearby is sucked into the middle of the wind which is called *the eye of the storm.*

The speed and strength of winds are measured by the Beaufort Scale. Look at the opposite page.

Try this

Is there a wind today?
Look outside. Is anything being moved by the wind?

Can you work out the wind speed by using the Beaufort Scale?

Hurricane

eye of the storm

Tornado

The Beaufort Scale

Force | Wind speed

1 **light air**　　　　$1\frac{1}{2}$-5 km/h
Smoke drifts gently but wind vanes don't move.

2 **light breeze**　　　　6-11 km/h
Wind felt on face, wind vanes begin to move, leaves rustle.

3 **gentle breeze**　　　12-20 km/h
Leaves and small twigs constantly moving, light flags will blow in the breeze.

4 **moderate breeze**　　21-29 km/h
Dust and leaves blown above the ground, small branches move.

5 **fresh breeze**　　　30-39 km/h
Small, leafy trees sway.

6 **strong breeze**　　　40-50 km/h
Large branches sway, umbrellas turn inside out.

7 **moderate gale**　　　51-61 km/h
Whole trees in motion, people have to push against the wind when they walk.

8 **fresh gale**　　　62-74 km/h
Twigs break off trees, it's difficult to walk.

9 **strong gale**　　　75-87 km/h
Chimney pots and slates on roofs can be blown away.

10 **whole gale**　　　88-101 km/h
Houses badly damaged, trees uprooted.

11 **storm**　　　102-117 km/h
Usually at sea, very high waves and much damage.

12 **hurricane**　　above 117 km/h
Countryside flattened, houses and trees blown away.

Temperature

Temperature is the word we use to describe how hot or cold something is. The earth is heated by the sun so the temperature anywhere on earth will depend on the number of sunlight hours each day. The summer season usually has the highest temperatures. Wind and clouds can alter the temperature. Even if the sun is shining a cold wind can blow. This can reduce the temperature. When there are clouds in the sky, the sunlight can be stopped from reaching the earth with full strength. This also reduces the temperature.

The weather has always played an important part in people's lives. How will the weather affect the food being grown? Is it safe to be out at sea or is there a storm coming? What sort of clothes do we need to wear?

The study of the weather is called *meteorology*. Today, meteorologists use many instruments including computers, to record and forecast the weather. These instruments are used on ships and man-made satellites, as well as on land. Weather forecasts are given daily all round the world in newspapers and on radio and television. Here are some of the instruments used by meteorologists. Try to find out what each of them is used to measure.

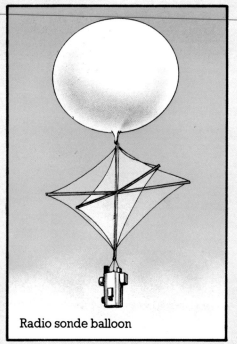

Radio sonde balloon

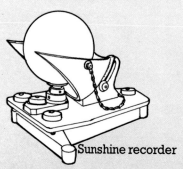

Sunshine recorder

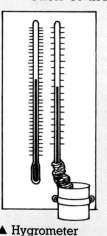

▲ Hygrometer

▼ Rain gauge

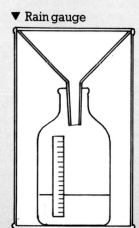

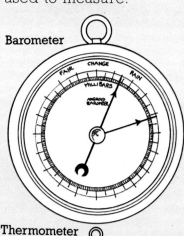

Barometer

Thermometer

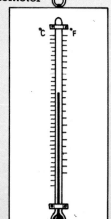

You may not have all these instruments but you can still keep a simple weather record. You could use a chart like this. This example is only filled in for three days. You could keep a record for a whole week, or longer.

Date	Tuesday 3rd March	Wednesday 4th March	Thursday 5th March
Time 8am			
2pm			

Key
Some of the symbols in this key have been used on the chart above. You could make your own key and use some different symbols.

Sun

Frost

Dew

Mist

Rain

Cloud see page 20

Wind see page 23 eg.

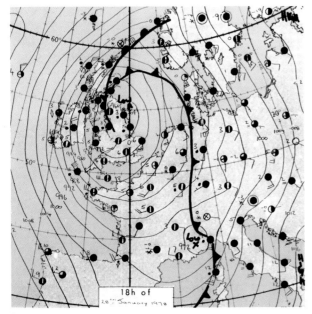

Weather map

If you do have weather instruments, you can use them to give more information on your record. For example, if you have a rain gauge, you can work out how much rain there has been every day.

The weather is different in different parts of the world, and at different times of the year. The temperature and the amount of sun in one place alters as the earth orbits the sun. Near the North and South Poles there is always snow and ice. Near the equator it is always too hot for this. The strongest winds and the heaviest rains are found near the equator.

Seas and oceans

Different weather conditions build up in the atmosphere and the seasons change as the earth orbits the sun. These things affect the water covering the earth's surface as well as the land.

The areas of water are called *seas* and *oceans*. They have names in the same way as areas of land do.

Sometimes seas are completely enclosed by land. The Caspian Sea is like this. Oceans are larger than seas. There are five oceans.

Look at the oceans on this map and read their names. Look at the seas too. There is only room to mark a few of the seas. You will find others if you look at an atlas. You will see that there is more water than land covering the earth.

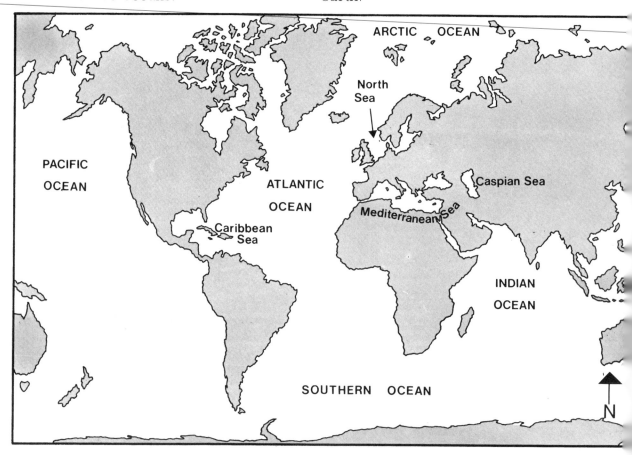

Saltiness

Most lakes and rivers are not salty. We say they are *fresh water*.

The waters in the seas and oceans are salty. Some are more salty than others. Where it is hot and sunny with little rain, the water is usually very salty. This is because water evaporates. The water vapour rises into the atmosphere (see page 18). The salt is left behind.

If there is a lot of rain, sea water is *diluted*. It becomes less salty. This also happens where large rivers flow into seas and oceans. The fresh water from the rivers dilutes the salty water. There are plants and animals which only live in the salty seas and oceans. They are called *marine* plants and animals.

A river flowing into the sea

Movement
Waves

Seas and oceans are liquid. This means they can move fairly easily. You can nearly always see waves on the water surface. They may be so small that they are like ripples. But if they are whipped up by gales and storms, the waves may be as tall as houses. Sometimes the crests of waves (the tops) make surf as they splash down.

A lifeboat on stormy sea

Currents

Waves move water to and fro but not over long distances. It is the ocean currents which do this. The currents carry water up and down and round and round. The water moves in huge circles over the earth's surface. Temperatures and winds help to move the water. Sometimes land is in the way which makes the water change direction. Currents of warm water, like the Gulf Stream, bring warmth to the places they pass through. Cold currents do the opposite.

This map shows the warm and cold currents in the seas and oceans. Warm currents are shown in pink and cold currents are shown in blue

Tides

Waves move surface water. Ocean currents move large amounts of water over long distances. Tides move the seas and oceans in and out over the edge of the land.

Tides are caused by the moon with the sun's help. As the moon travels round the earth, it pulls the seas and oceans towards it. This is because of the force of *gravity*. The water is pulled towards the moon and falls back again as the moon moves on. When the water is pulled up over the land, it is *high tide*. When it falls right back, it is *low tide*. The tide usually comes in and out twice each day.

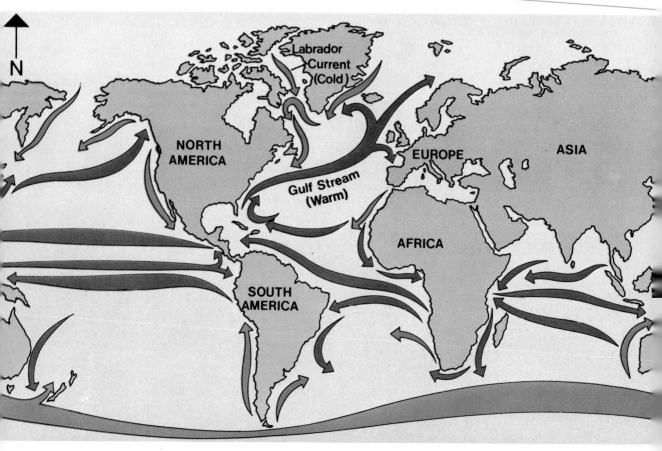

Land movement

You now know that the seas and oceans move about on the earth's surface. The land moves, too, only very gradually. There is also movement inside the earth.

Millions of years ago, the land and oceans were in different places. The changes on the surface of the earth still go on. If we could see into the future, perhaps ten million years ahead, our planet wouldn't look like it does now. Some mountains may be higher; streams and rivers may be in different places. It is hard to imagine how these changes take place because they happen so slowly, over millions of years.

To understand what is happening, you need to know what is inside the earth.

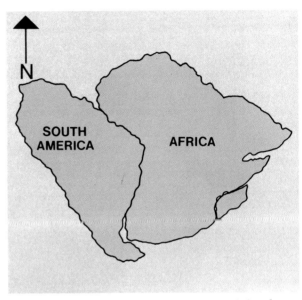

South America and Africa were once joined

South America and Africa are now separate

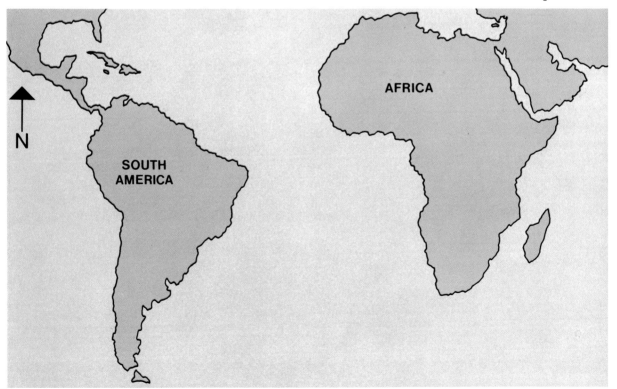

What is our planet made of?

If you look around, you will see what covers the surface of the earth. There is soil, sand, water, plants and animals – including people. There are also many things which have been made by people – buildings, machines and roads. These things are all on top of the earth. What is underneath them? Is the earth solid or hollow? Is it hot or cold under the surface? Is it hard right through or is there liquid inside?

This is how the earth would look if a slice was cut out of it. There are three parts to our planet: the *core*, the *mantle* and the *crust*.

The core is at the centre of the earth. It is extremely hot there. It's difficult to know exactly what the core is like because it is so far inside the earth. The edge of the core is nearly 3000km from the surface. A car moving at 100km/h would take 30 hours to travel that far!

The mantle is also very hot. It has rocks inside it. Some of these rocks have melted because they are so hot. They are liquid instead of solid. The liquid is called *magma*. It has minerals and gases in it, including water vapour. The magma is in the lower part of the mantle. The upper mantle is cooler. It is nearer the earth's surface. The rocks are solid there.

The *crust* is the part of the earth that we know most about. It is made of solid rocks. People who study these rocks are called *geologists*. The crust is the thinnest part of the earth. It is not nearly as thick as the mantle or core. The crust is usually between 35km and 50km thick.

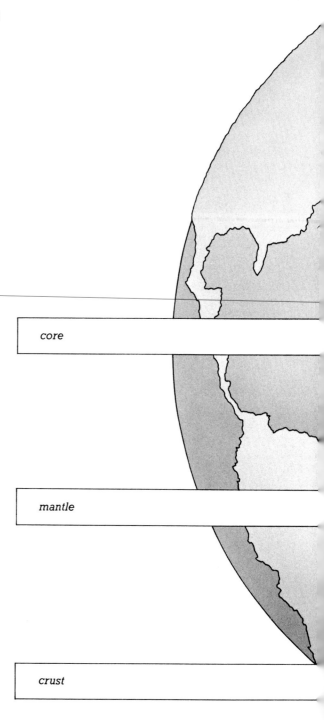

core

mantle

crust

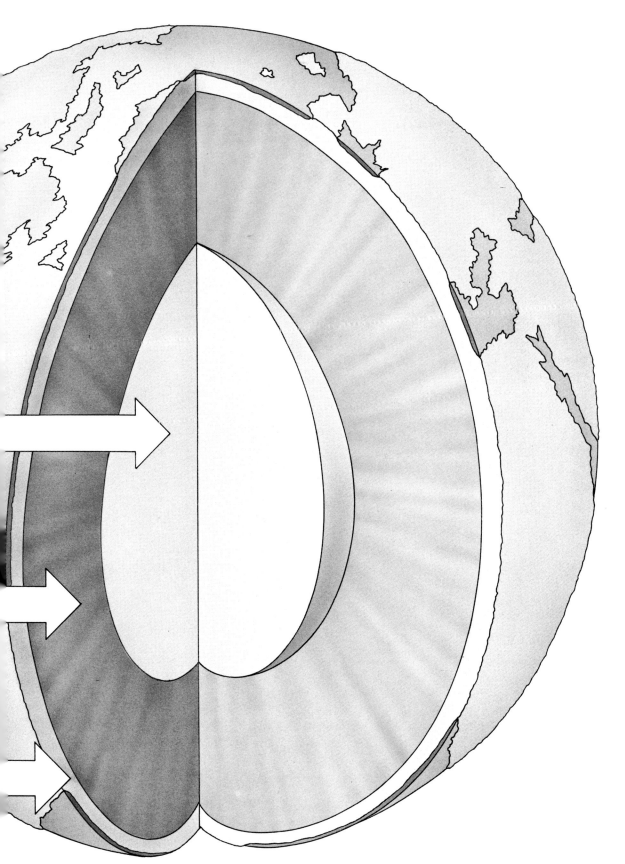

Old Faithful geyser, USA

There are a few places where the crust is thin – only a few kilometres deep. Cracks in thin parts of the crust sometimes fill with water. The water is then heated by the mantle. The water gets so hot that it boils over. Steam and hot water come out from the ground through *hot springs* and *geysers*. There are hot springs and geysers in Iceland, USA and New Zealand. The earth's crust is also thin under the deepest parts of the oceans.

Rocks

Many of the rocks which make the earth's crust are hidden. They are buried underneath soil or water. But sometimes they can be seen. Look at these photographs of bare rock. Look at the different colours and shapes.

Rocks feel different from each other, too. It's easy to think all rocks are very hard. But some rocks are softer than others. Chalk and limestone are soft rocks. They seem firm to the touch but are easily worn away. Granite is extremely hard. It is often used to make kerbstones because it is so hard.

Slate quarry ▲

▼ Limestone hills   Basalt cliffs ▶

You now know that there are different sorts of rocks. The earth's crust is not the same all over. There are three types of rock in it. Each type is made in a different way. The three types are called *igneous*, *sedimentary* and *metamorphic* rocks.

Igneous rocks

These are sometimes called fire rocks. This is because they are made in great heat inside the earth. These rocks were once so hot that they were liquid. They were the magma inside the mantle. As the liquid moved nearer to the earth's surface, it cooled. As it cooled it turned to stone. Over three quarters of the earth's crust is made of igneous rocks. Most of these are hidden under the sea.

Sedimentary rocks

These are made in water on top of the earth. They are made from sludge which forms on the sea bed (the bottom of the sea). The sludge is made from millions of tiny pieces of rock and animal remains. Sediment is the word used to describe the muddy sludge.

The tiny pieces of rock have been washed from the land into streams and rivers and then carried into the sea. The animal remains in the sediment are very small. They are tiny pieces of shells and skeletons of sea creatures.

▲ Basalt (an igneous rock)

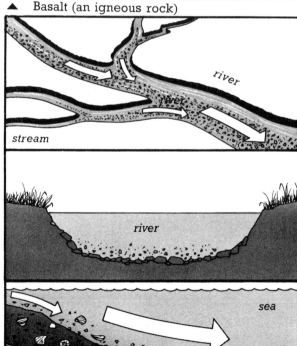

These diagrams show how sediment is carried by streams and rivers into the sea. The arrows show the way the sediment moves ▶

Gradually the sediment on the sea bed gets thicker. It gets heavier too. The sediment at the bottom is compressed, or packed together. After millions of years it turns into rock.

Sedimentary rocks are always soft rocks. They are built up in layers, called *strata*. These layers look like stripes in the rock. There are sedimentary rocks on land. But remember they were made under the sea. This means that seas once covered the land where these rocks are found.

Sandstone (a sedimentary rock)

Metamorphic rocks

These are rocks made from other rocks. They are very hard. Metamorphic rocks are made from igneous and sedimentary rocks. When these rocks are heated and put under pressure, they change. They become metamorphic rocks. These can be made inside or on top of the earth. Chalk and limestone are sedimentary rocks which are changed by heat and pressure into a metamorphic rock called marble.

Marble (a metamorphic rock)

How mountains are made

People now believe that the earth's crust is not in one piece. It isn't a whole, complete skin round the outside of the planet. Instead, it is made up of huge pieces called *plates*. These fit together like pieces of a jigsaw puzzle. The movement of the earth makes the plates slide about on top of it (but only very slightly – you wouldn't be able to see this happening). When two plates slide into each other, pressure builds up between them. What do you think happens then?

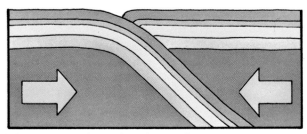

The arrows show that these plates are moving towards each other

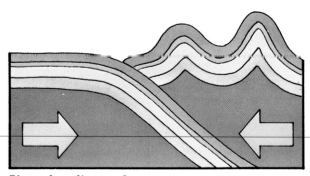

Plates bending under pressure

Try this

Take two slabs of fairly soft plasticine. Push them together so they touch each other. Keep pushing them slowly together from the outside edges. What is happening to the plasticine in the middle?

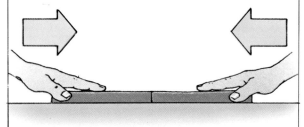

Mountains such as the Himalays were probably made like this. The rocks were wrinkled and pushed up over millions of years. This happened because two plates bumped into each other and pressure built up between them.

Himalayan mountains

Volcanoes

There is also pressure inside the earth. It is strong enough to break the earth's crust and to move rocks in the crust. This is what happens when there are volcanoes and earthquakes.

Look at this diagram to see what happens when a volcano erupts.

Pressure has built up inside the earth. Magma has burst through a weak spot in the earth's crust. The hole which is made is called a *vent*. The liquid rock is called *lava*. When the lava pours out of the volcano, it begins to cool. It turns into rock. It becomes igneous rock. New rock has been made. At the same time, the heat of the magma is changing some of the old rock into metamorphic rock.

This is happening both inside the volcano and where the lava comes out of it. You can see this in the diagram.

Can you see how some of the magma has gone sideways? It hasn't all gone up through the vent.

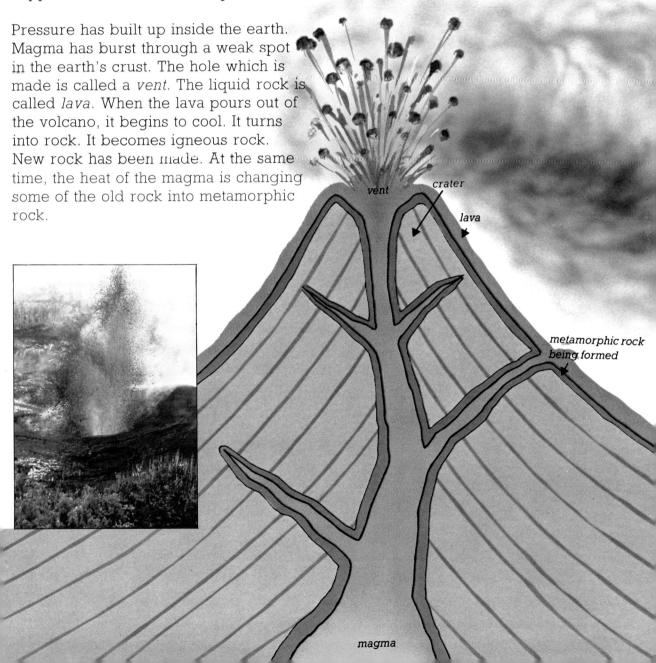

vent

crater

lava

metamorphic rock being formed

magma

It is very hard to imagine a heat great enough to melt rocks and change them. See if you can work out the temperature of some of the magma. When a volcano erupts, magma comes from 3000km inside the earth. The temperature goes up 1°C for every kilometre inside the earth. So what will the temperature be at 3000km deep? What is the temperature of boiling water? How many times hotter will the magma be?

Have another look at the photograph on page 37. Just before an eruption like this, there is a loud rumbling noise. Imagine the roar of a football crowd and loud thunder together, going on and on and on. This is a very small sound compared to the sound which some volcanoes make.

There is rumbling and shaking. The pressure builds up to bursting point. Suddenly the volcano begins to erupt. First of all, gases are forced out of the vent. Some of these may be poisonous. After the gas comes dust, ashes and lava. As the lava pours down the sides of the volcano, more ash and rocks may be blown into the air. Some lava cools enough to become rock as it blows through the air. Pumice stone is formed like this.

When a volcano erupts, it is very dangerous. Eruptions are often so sudden that people living near the volcano do not have time to escape.

Gas cloud from Mount Pelée volcano

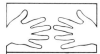

See if you can buy a piece of pumice stone from the chemist. Some people use pumice stone to rub dirt and stains off their skin when they wash.

Notice the weight of your pumice stone. Is it lighter or heavier than a garden stone of the same size? Look at the pumice stone through a magnifying lens. Can you see anything which would affect its weight?

Pumice stone has changed very quickly from lava to stone – so quickly that the gas bubbles in it did not have time to escape. Pumice stone is like a froth which has turned to stone.

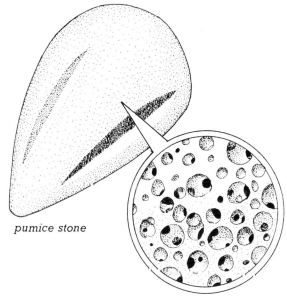

pumice stone

pumice stone magnified

Different types of volcanoes and lava

Some volcanoes are cone shaped. As the lava pours out, it builds up the sides of the *crater*. The sides get higher and higher. Eventually the sides of the cone crack. Lava can then escape through these cracks as well.

Some lava is runny and pours away very quickly. It can travel a long way from the volcano, destroying vegetation and people's homes. Some lava is thick and moves slowly.

Some volcanoes are not cone shaped. The lava from these overflows gradually, instead of exploding. People are not often killed by these volcanoes.

Lava which has cooled and hardened

Active, dormant and extinct are words which we use to describe volcanoes. If they are active, they can erupt at any time. Lava comes from them.

Dormant volcanoes are sleeping. They will erupt again at some time. This will happen when enough pressure builds up underneath them. Dormant volcanoes often erupt without any warning. They may have been asleep for years and years between eruptions

Mount St Helens in North America was a dormant volcano, but now it is active again. Before it erupted in 1980, the volcano had only erupted five times in the last five hundred years.

Extinct volcanoes are dead. They erupted in the past but will not do so again. This is because the pressure inside the earth has changed. There is no longer enough pressure to make the volcano erupt.

Volcanoes can be on land or in the sea. Sometimes a volcano will make a new island. This happens when there is enough lava to build up above the water. Surtsey, off the coast of Iceland, is an island like this.

Volcanoes are found in hot and cold lands. It is the magma and lava which are hot, not the climate of the area.

How a volcanic island is formed in the sea

1. A volcano erupts in the sea

2. Lava pours out and builds up

3. Lava hardens and the volcano stops erupting
4. Hardened lava becomes a new island in the sea

Earthquakes

Damage caused by an earthquake in Guatemala, Central America

The damage in this picture was caused by an earthquake. The ground under the buildings actually moved. It shook everything above the ground and caused chaos. Many people die in earthquakes and complete cities can be destroyed.

Earthquakes happen in parts of the world where there is a lot of movement in the earth's crust. An example of such an area is California.

Do you remember that we said the crust of the earth is made of plates? (See page 36.) In California, two of these plates meet. They form what is known as a *fault*. This is a crack hundreds of miles long in the surface of the earth.

On one side of the fault, one plate is moving northwards. The other plate is moving southwards. Most of the time they move fairly smoothly past each other but sometimes there is a sudden jerk in the movement. This causes an earthquake.

California often has small earthquakes and there was a very big one in 1906 which destroyed the city of San Francisco. The vibrations caused by an earthquake travel for many kilometres.

Usually we only hear about big earthquakes in the news when people have been killed, but there are very many small earthquakes, perhaps as many as one million a year. Many of them happen under the sea. Earthquakes show us that the forces which move land and make mountains are still in action.

Erosion

Igneous and metamorphic rocks are the hardest and strongest rocks. But even they aren't strong enough to last for ever. They are attacked by weather and water – streams, rivers and the sea. *Erosion* is the word we use to describe this.

Look at this photograph of some cliffs Once they looked like one unbroken piece of rock. But now they have been eroded. They have been worn away and pieces have been broken off. The boulders and stones you can see at the bottom of the cliffs were once part of one piece of rock. How are rocks eroded like this?

Erosion by the weather

Rain, frost, sun and wind can all attack rocks and erode them.

Water falls on rock as rain, snow, frost or dew. The rock is worn down as water runs over it. When it rains, water seeps into cracks in the rock. When the water freezes it becomes ice and expands (gets bigger). The ice acts like a wedge in the cracks. It makes the cracks grow larger and larger until pieces of rock break off.

The sun can also crack rocks. The heat of the sun makes rock expand. At night, when the rock cools down, it contracts (gets smaller). These changes in temperature make the rock crack. This often happens in the desert.

The wind also erodes rock. It cannot do this on its own, but when the wind blows, it sometimes picks up sharp pieces of sand. This wears the rocks away – a little like sandpaper would! The rocks in the picture below have been eroded by the sun and wind.

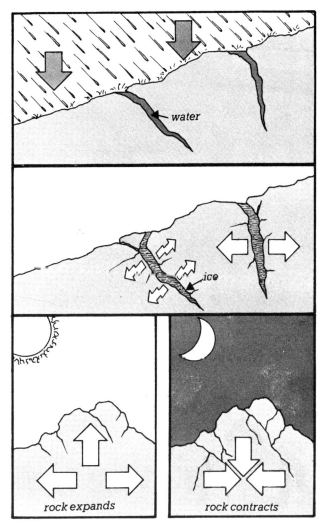

water

ice

rock expands

rock contracts

Erosion by water

Look at the photograph of the Grand Canyon in North America. Can you see a river at the bottom?

The river is eroding the rock as it moves along. It is carrying away tiny bits of rock. Gradually, the river has cut deeper and deeper into the ground. The river has eroded the rocks over millions of years. Find the name of the river in an atlas.

The sea can also erode rocks. The cliffs in the picture below have been worn down by the waves.

▲ Grand Canyon

How caves, arches and stacks are made

Every time the sea washes against the coast, it wears away the land. When there are storms, waves pound the cliffs and rocks. These waves often carry stones and boulders which are smashed against the land. The softest parts of the land are eroded faster because they are weaker than the harder parts. This means that erosion can change the shape of coastlines.

Caves

Sometimes the sea cuts right inside rocks and cliffs. It makes a hole. Gradually, the hole gets bigger as more rock is eroded. The hole becomes a *cave*. Some caves are very large.

Arches are made in the same way as caves. Look at the one in the photograph. It was once solid rock. The sea has eroded the soft parts and left an arch.

Arch

What do you think eventually happens to arches? They collapse because the sea continues to erode them. When an arch falls down, the side of it is often left like the ones in this photograph.

It is then called a *stack*. Even stacks vanish in time. The sea washes round the bottoms, making them thinner and thinner. In the end, the stacks tumble down and are carried away by the sea. It takes many, many years for caves, arches and stacks to be made and broken down.

Stacks

Erosion by ice

The picture on the right shows a valley with a *glacier* in it. A glacier is a slowly moving mass of ice. Thousands of years ago, in the Ice Ages, large areas of land were covered by glaciers. As the ice melted, it slid down the hills and mountains and through the valleys. Because the ice was heavy and solid, it knocked the sharp edges off the rocks underneath it. The glacier carried away the broken pieces of rock. These then wore down other rocks as they went. Sometimes they left scratches on the rocks.

Have another look at the picture on the right. When the glacier has finally gone, the part of the valley it filled will be smooth and U-shaped.

▲ Glacier

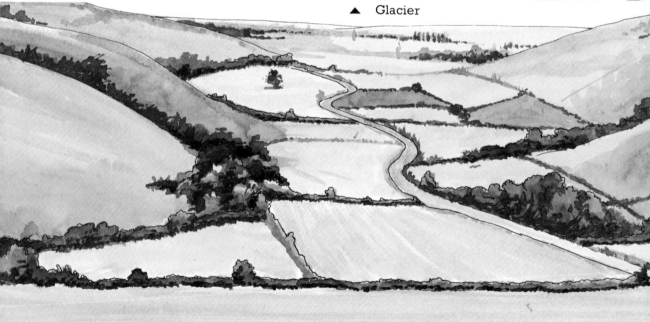

The hills and valleys in the picture above were once covered with glaciers. Look at their shape. They are rounded. The land is smooth, not jagged.

Chemical erosion

Some rocks can be dissolved by chemicals carried in water. This picture shows a limestone cave. Water containing carbon dioxide has run through the rock and dissolved part of it. There are now tunnels and caves where there used to be rock. Sometimes there are underground rivers and lakes where the rock has been dissolved like this.

Look at the cave again. Can you see spikes? They are hanging from the roof of the cave and also sticking up from the floor. These spikes are called stalactites and stalagmites. They were formed after the cave was hollowed out.

Water ran through the limestone and dissolved some of it. Some of the water formed drops on the cave roof. Then the water evaporated, leaving behind tiny lumps of limestone. Over thousands of years, more drops formed on the lumps and evaporated. Slowly the lumps grew into stalactites.

While the stalactites were growing, more spikes were forming on the floor underneath. Some drips from the stalactites fell to the floor and evaporated, leaving lumps of limestone. As more water dripped, the lumps got bigger. They grew up from the floor of the cave. They grew into stalagmites. Stalagmites and stalactites go on growing until they meet to form pillars.

How do rock pieces move and settle?

Pieces that have broken off large rocks are often moved away. Some of the pieces are very small. They are like dust. Some of these can be blown away by the wind. Others are washed away. After heavy rain or snow, water runs over the land. It carries stones along with it. The water moves downhill and later joins a stream or river.

The water in the stream or river carries along its load of stones. Some stones are small; others are quite large. Rivers end at a lake or in the sea. They leave the stones there. Sea water is always moving, so the stones which go into the sea are carried on another journey.

What do you think happens to the pieces of rock and stone? Perhaps you can work it out by looking at these pictures.

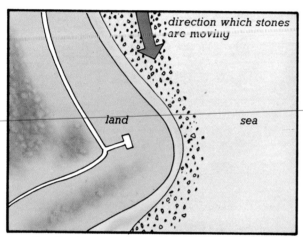

▲ Small stones and dust carried in water

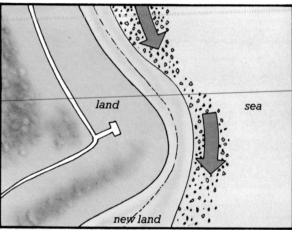

▲ They are dropped on the edge of the coast
▼ They gradually make new land

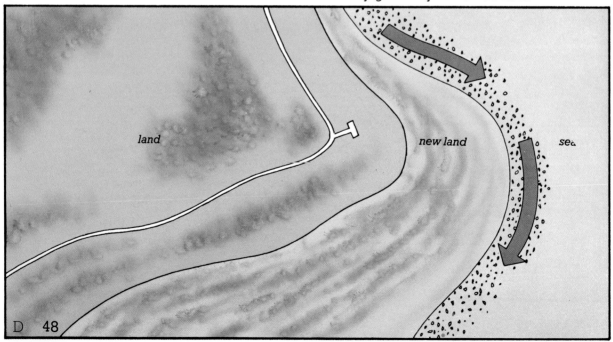

Some of the rock pieces are dropped on the sea bed. They mix with the bodies of tiny creatures. After millions of years the sludge which is made like this changes into sedimentary rock. More new rock is made. (Look back to page 34.)

Our earth is changing all the time. It is changing inside and outside. We may not notice much of this, because it all happens so slowly. But we can see signs that it is happening.

All the time, rocks are being eroded. Small pieces are moved by water and wind. They are then dropped on land or on the sea bed.

Sediment on the sea bed changes to rock after millions of years. Volcanoes and earthquakes tell us of movement inside the earth. Earthquakes can bend and crack rocks inside the earth. Eventually, even what goes on inside the earth can be seen. After millions of years of erosion, bent and cracked rocks are uncovered.

▲ Diagonal line is a crack (called a fault)

▼ Curved lines are bent rock (called folds)

What you can find in rocks

Fossils

Do you know the word *prehistoric?* It means 'before history'. History started when people began recording things with words and pictures. You have probably heard of dinosaurs. They were prehistoric animals. They lived millions of years ago. They are extinct now. This means that there aren't any dinosaurs alive any more.

How do we know about dinosaurs? Nothing was written down or drawn about them when they were alive. The information has come from fossils. Here are some fossils. There are shells, coral, a tree trunk and a bone.

Sometimes fossils are the actual bodies of living things which have been preserved. However, fossils are usually made of rock.

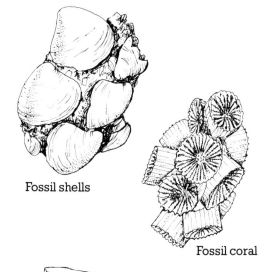

Fossil shells

Fossil coral

Fossil tree trunk

Dinosaur

Fossil bone

How fossils were made

When plants and animals die, their bodies rot. The soft parts of their bodies rot first. Bones and shells last longer but eventually they rot too. This happened to most prehistoric plants and animals. But some were saved. They were frozen in ice or buried in mud (sediment). Gradually, sediment filled spaces in the dead bodies as they rotted. The sediment turned into rock.

Ammonite fossil

Look at this photograph of an ammonite. An ammonite was a type of mollusc. (See *The Living Earth*, Part 1.) After the animal had been buried in mud, its body slowly rotted. As this happened, sediment filled the space that was left. The sediment eventually became rock. The ammonite became a fossil.

Fossils are usually only found in sedimentary rock. Igneous and metamorphic rocks are formed in great heat. This heat would destroy the plant and animal bodies before they could be changed to fossils.

How a fossil is made.

1. Animal at the bottom of the water.

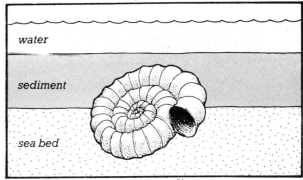

2. Gradually covered by sediment.

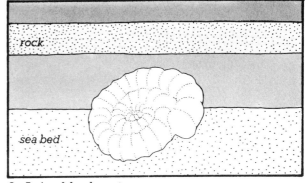

3. Animal body rots.

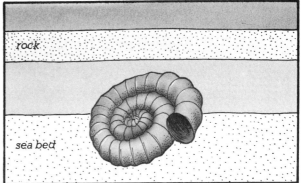

4. Space filled with sediment. Sediment changes to rock and a fossil is formed.

What fossils tell us

Fossils can tell us things which we can't learn from history books. They tell us about living things which existed millions of years ago. There are fossils which show us parts of living bodies. There are also fossilised foot prints. These are usually tracks which were made in mud before it changed to rock.

Scientists can tell how old rocks and fossils are. This means that we know when creatures lived as well as what they were like. The last dinosaurs lived over fifty million years ago. Fossils of sea creatures are often dug out of rocks on land. This tells us that the sea once covered that part of the earth. In this way, fossils can tell us where the seas and rivers were millions of years ago.

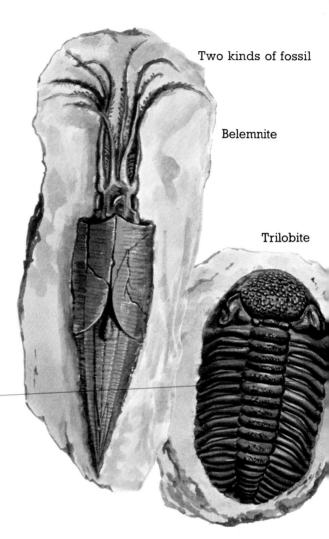

Two kinds of fossil

Belemnite

Trilobite

Fossil fuels

Coal, oil and gas are fossil fuels. We take them from the ground and from under the sea. They are made from the bodies of animals and plants which were once alive. We use fossil fuels faster than new ones are being made.

Oil platform

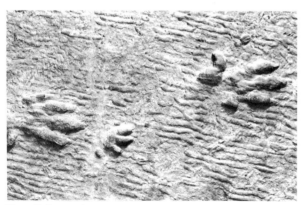

Fossil footprints

Crystals and minerals

You have thought about how rocks are made and which of them are soft or hard. But you haven't looked closely at different pieces of rock.

Look at the patterns on these rocks. Look at the shapes inside the patterns. Look at the different colours, too. How many colours are there in each rock?

The patterns and shapes are made by minerals. Most rocks are made from a collection of minerals.

Malachite

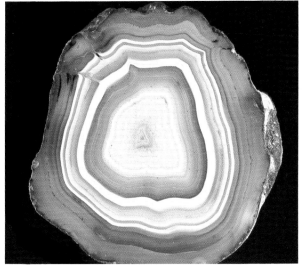

▲ Agate

▼ Marble

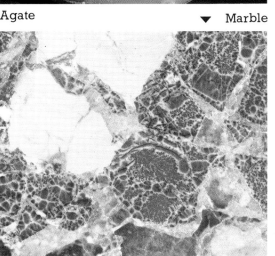

Cinnabar

All minerals come from the ground. They were once molten rock. As the liquid cooled, the minerals formed crystals which joined together. If the liquid cooled quickly, the crystals are small. If the liquid cooled slowly, the rock has large crystals. This happens when magma changes to rock inside the earth. Crystals can be different shapes. It depends which mineral they are made from.

Minerals are found in rocks, sand, soil and the sea. Some have metals in them, others do not. We could not live without them. We use minerals all the time. We eat them, wear them and use them to build with.

Not all minerals can be used straight from the ground. Some of them have to be cleaned and purified. These are refined minerals. We get iron ore from the ground but it isn't iron until it has been refined. Most iron is turned into steel. This is much stronger than iron.

Different minerals come from different parts of the world. We use minerals much faster than new ones are being made.

Quartz crystals

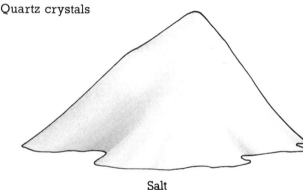

Salt

Diamond ring

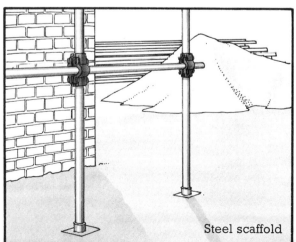

Steel scaffold

Soil

Soil is something which nearly everyone has seen and touched. We know that things grow in it. But what is soil? How was it made? Why is it different colours in different places? Why do different things grow in different soils?

Soil is made from rocks and humus and has air and water in it. You already know how pieces break off large rocks (see page 42). Now try this to find out how these pieces change to soil.

(see page 42)

Try this

Take some lumps of clay which have dried out. They must be really hard. Hold the lumps and bang them together. What happens? Pick up the smaller bits and rub them together between your hands. What happens now?

Soil isn't made by hand. Rocks are crumbled into smaller pieces by erosion. The crumbled pieces of rock are moved by wind and water. These pieces make part of the soil.

There is also *humus* in soil. Humus is made from rotting plants and animals. They have rotted so much that you can't see the separate bits. Humus is *organic*. This means it is made from living things.

Soil being prepared for crop planting

Look at this diagram. It shows us what soil is like if we cut through it. At the top, there is *topsoil* which has a lot of humus. Below it there is *subsoil* which has less humus. (We say it is less rich.) Below the subsoil is rock. Plants need sunlight and carbon dioxide from the air to make them grow. (See *The Living Earth*, Part 1.) But they also need water and other substances which they absorb from the soil through their roots. When plants die, they rot and eventually turn back into humus. This releases the substances which the plant took out of the soil. This means that more plants can grow in the soil or, in other words, the soil remains *fertile*.

The particles of rock in soil can be different sizes. Sandy soil has bigger particles than clay. Clay can hold more water, so it feels sticky. The most fertile soil is loam which is a mixture of clay and sandy soil.

Soil can also be different colours. The minerals in soil give it its colour.

This diagram shows what soil is like if we cut through it

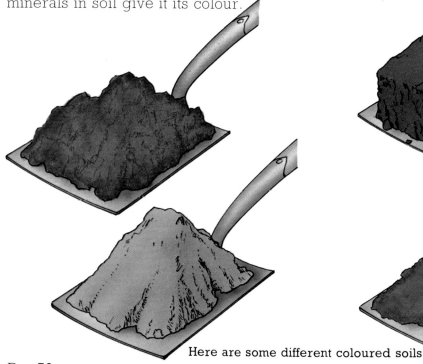

Here are some different coloured soils

Soil is one of the most important things which we have on our earth. Soil feeds plants and plants are eaten by animals. Plants and animals are eaten by us. If there was no soil, there would be nothing for us to eat.

Look at the top picture. Lots of different plants and animals can live in this area. The soil is fertile and fairly flat. This area also has good amounts of sun and rain to provide warmth, light and water.

Look at this desert. Very few plants are able to grow here. The soil is sandy and the weather is very hot. There is very little humus in the soil. For most of the year, there is no rain. When the rain comes, it is very heavy and washes away most of the useful substances in the soil.

We call this type of land *tundra.* It is very cold here and there is only a thin layer of soil. For part of the year the soil is frozen and covered with snow, so nothing can grow. The tops of mountains are usually like this, too.

There are plants growing here but the soil is not good. This is a swamp where the ground is *waterlogged* (full of water). The water cannot drain away. When soil is soaked with water like this, there is hardly any air in it. Only a few kinds of plants are able to survive these conditions.

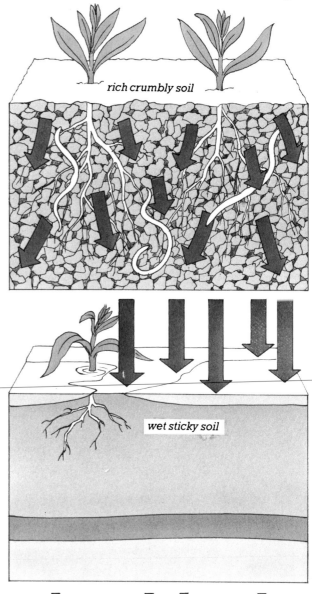

Fertile soil must have the right mixture of rock particles, humus, air and water. This diagram shows what is needed. The soil is rich and crumbly. Between the crumbs of soil there are spaces for air. The spaces also make it possible for water to filter through. This stops the soil becoming waterlogged. Plant roots find it easy to grow in and out between the crumbs of soil.

This is what happens in clay, where the soil is too wet and too sticky. The tiny particles of soil stick together as a lump. There are very few spaces and it is difficult for roots to grow into the soil. Water cannot drain through soil like this. If there is a lot of rain the water soaks the soil and then makes puddles on top. If the rain goes on and on, the puddles grow and join up. This is what happens when land floods.

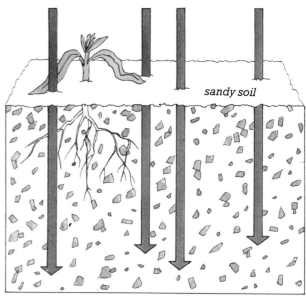

The opposite is happening in this diagram. The soil is sandy. There are plenty of air holes and it is easy for roots to grow. But water runs straight through because there is nothing to absorb it. This type of soil is always dry. It is usually poor, too, because the water washes away the goodness in it. This is what happens in deserts.

Rotting organic material (a compost heap)

Looking after good soil

Good soil is very valuable and there is not enough of it for our needs. We have already built houses and factories on a lot of the land. If we take plants out of the soil for food, then no humus is returned to the soil and it becomes less fertile.

The goodness which plants take out of the soil has to be replaced. This is done with *fertilisers*. Gardeners and farmers spread these on the soil to make it fertile. Natural fertilisers are *organic*. This means they are made from things which were once alive. Chemical fertilisers are made in factories.

Gardeners and farmers also care for the soil in other ways. When they dig, plough, and break up the soil, they are putting air back into it. They are also making it crumbly. In some places, there is not enough rain for part or all of the year. To grow crops, the soil must be *irrigated*. Water is taken from rivers, dams, lakes or wells and sprayed on to the growing plants. Soil that is too wet can be drained using ditches and drainage pipes.

▲ Spreading chemical fertilizer
▼ Part of the Aswan dam, Egypt

Protecting the soil

Wind and water can carry away the valuable topsoil. They erode it. The sea also erodes the land when it beats against the coast. (See page 45.)

These pictures show how the soil can be protected against such attacks.

1 The marram grass and pine trees have been planted to hold the sand in place. Their roots do this. If the plants were not there the wind would blow the sand where it wasn't wanted.

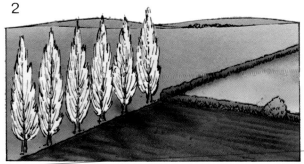

2 Rows of trees are often planted to act as wind-breaks. They reduce the strength of the wind so that it isn't strong enough to carry soil away. Hedges do this too.

3 Banks and walls are built beside rivers and seas to stop flooding. The flood waters cannot then carry the soil away with them.

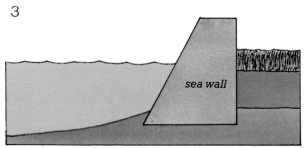

sea wall

Reclaiming the soil

Sometimes it is possible to make more soil useful. The sea carries soil away but it drops soil too. Eventually a new piece of coastline grows. The marshes in this picture were made like this. Now grass grows on the marshes and sheep can graze there.

With the help of science we could perhaps grow food where the soil is now poor. Deserts could be irrigated. Frozen ground could be heated. Forests and swamps could be cleared and drained. But this would take time and enormous amounts of money.

Reclaimed land (Romney Marsh, Britain)

What will happen to our planet?

It has taken millions of years for our planet to form and develop and the earth goes on changing. The plates on its surface are gradually moving. (See page 36.) New mountains and valleys are being made and old ones being worn away. Coasts are eroded and built up in different places. These changes are happening naturally. There are other changes that are being made by humans. The earth's natural supplies (resources) are being used up.

Humans, like the earth, have developed over millions of years. In the Stone Age humans used caves for their homes and hunted for food. They built fires to cook over and to give heat. They gathered wood for fuel. There was enough food and fuel for everyone. As hundreds and hundreds of years went by, humans became builders and farmers. They took iron ore and other minerals from the ground. They developed new skills and learned how to use the earth's natural resources. Eventually, complicated machines were invented to do a lot of the work.

We have now left the Stone Age far behind. We are living in the age of computers. But we still need food and fuel. The fuel gives us the energy which powers our tools and machines. Coal, oil and gas are the fuels we use most.

Think about all the machines which we use in our homes. Energy is needed to make all these machines work, and minerals from the ground are needed to make them. Can you think of any other things in your home which use energy? Do you know which fuel is burnt to make that energy? It may not be the same fuel for all the machines.

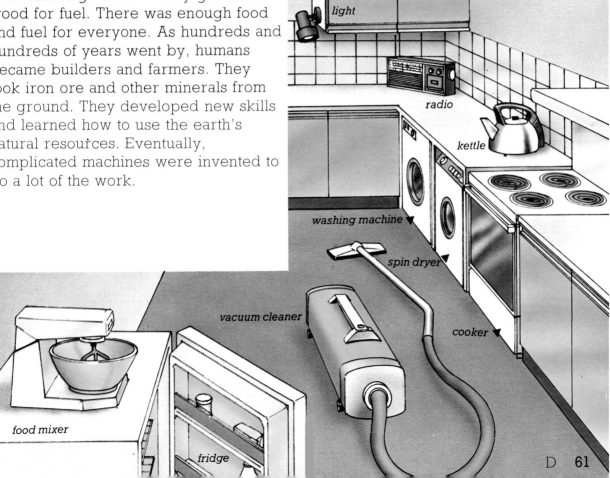

light

radio

kettle

washing machine ▼

spin dryer ▼

vacuum cleaner

cooker ▼

food mixer

fridge

There are now over four thousand billion people living on our planet. Land, fuels and minerals are being used up very quickly.

Land

Every year there are more and more people living on the earth. Extra space is needed for houses and factories, and for growing food. As we use more land there is less left for wild plants and animals. If we take their homes, they will not all survive. Many will become extinct.

Fossil fuels

Energy is being used all the time. It is used in our homes and where people work. It is used to power transport, too. It is even needed to collect the fuels which provide our energy. A lot of energy is needed to build and run oil rigs, for example. Energy is also needed to carry the fuel to where it will be used. The earth's supplies of coal, oil and gas are running out.

Minerals

Look again at the machines on page 61. Minerals were used to make parts in all of them. Most of our machinery is made from minerals. What would we do without machines? They have become part of our lives. Fuels for energy could not be collected without machinery. But there isn't an unending supply of minerals. These too will eventually be used up.

What will happen if we use up all the land, fossil fuels and minerals? Perhaps we could learn to live without machines but we would still need shelter, food and warmth. All living things need these to survive. What about using Stone Age methods? We could hunt and build fires. But think carefully. Could we do that? If all the land is used by people there will be no wild plants and animals to hunt. There will not be enough wood to burn as fuel. What will happen to all the people? Will there be enough caves to shelter in? They would not be much good without food and warmth.

Looking after our planet

Land

If we can control the increase in the number of people on our planet, land could be saved. There would be room for wild plants and animals too. We cannot kill people but we can try to plan how many children are born.

Fossil fuels

Energy is needed but it does not always have to come from fossil fuels. Other ways are being developed and used. The fewer fossil fuels we use, the longer they will last. Here are some other ways of making energy.

1 Hydro-electric dam. The movement of water is the power used here.
2 Geysers (see page 32) can be used to give heat and energy. This is called geothermal power.
3 Nuclear power stations use a mineral called uranium to make energy. Unfortunately they also make radio-active waste materials. These can seriously harm living things unless they are handled very carefully. Many people feel that nuclear power stations should not be built.

4 There is a lot of power in the sun, wind, waves, and tides. In the future, these may be used to supply more energy.

Minerals

Look at the picture of a rubbish tip. There are all sorts of things on it. They have been thrown away because they are old, broken or no longer needed. Many of them have been made from minerals. Some of these things could be used again. They could be *recycled* This means they could be used to make new things. Have you seen a bottle bank in your nearest town? Bottles which are put inside are melted and made into new ones. Metals can also be melted and used again. Recycling means we can re-use some minerals. Perhaps in the future we shall save and recycle all sorts of things. Our rubbish may one day become very valuable.

Have you heard this word before . . . CONSERVATION? It means to save and care for. Our earth will last longer if we look after it and save its natural resources.

Index

This Index will help you to find some of the important things in The Living Earth, Part 4. Some of the page numbers about a subject are more important than others. These are shown in **dark letters.**